D0890014

First published in 1905
First published by V&A Publishing, 2011
This edition published 2014

Victoria and Albert Museum
South Kensington
London SW7 2RL
www.vandapublishing.com

Book design © V&A Publishing, 2014

The moral right of the author(s) has been asserted.

Hardback edition
ISBN 978 1 85177 788 4

10 9 8 7 6 5 4 3 2 1
2018 2017 2016 2015 2014

Cover design by here www.heredesign.co.uk

Printed in China

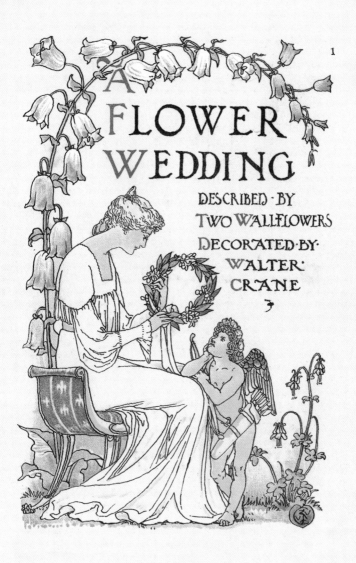

A FLOWER WEDDING

DESCRIBED · BY
TWO WALLFLOWERS

DECORATED · BY·
WALTER·
CRANE

Yes, flower bells rang right merry that day,
When there was a marriage of flowers,
they say.

Young LAD'S LOVE had courted Miss Meadow. Sweet,
And the two soon agreed at the Altar
to meet.

A LILY white robe was worn by the And { Bride, SWEET WILLIAM, the Groom, drest in red, at her side.

Miss VIOLET, PRIMROSE, and gay MARYGOLD,
With their LADIES' FINGERS her train did uphold.

In LADYSMOCKS, Bridesmaids, FORGET·ME·NOT blue,
With their sashes all tied in LOVE·KNOT·TRUE.

The Bride's Mother follows with loving EYEBRIGHT,
All in WINTER GREEN and fine FURZE bedight.

Whilst her father looked young, though
with OLD MAN'S BEARD.

(Was a DANDELION in youth I have heard.)

The troth was plighted for woe or
for weal,
And the lines attested by SOLOMON'S
SEAL:

The BACHELOR'S BUTTON was cast aside,

And the throng that witnessed was LONDON'S PRIDE:

There was GOOD KING HENRY, & tall
JONQUIL,

2

Like NARCISSUS himself by the waters still;

There were LORDS & LADIES to grace the dance,

And ROSE MARY, and—

ROSE·LA·FRANCE:

With his Golden Rod

the SWEET SULTAN came;

Lastly, CREEPING JENNY, an elderly dame

To order the feast_there was LING,
and HARTSTONGUE,

And Goosefoot with SAGE, the HOUSE-LEEK among

Very Sweet Peas, & Good Cherry Pie,
Such a feast as an Alderman could not deny!

In lovely KING·CUPS there was CHAMOMILE TEA

And the fortune in gifts was a wonder to see!
A new
PENNY-ROYAL,
A fine GOLDEN
FEATHER;

A pair of HORSE-CHESTNUTS,

a JACOB'S LADDER,

a fine ARROW-HEAD
Discovered long since in the river's
bed;

Garments of FLAX,

and a LADY's CUSHION;

HOSE-IN-HOSE, LADY'S SLIPPERS to put on,

BUTTERCUPS gold, and a PITCHER-
Nay, everything that a house PLANT,
could want.

I n VENUS'S·FLY·TRAP the pair drove away,

"SPEEDWELL, and be happy," their friends gaily say;

But alack! what a hubbub when one chanced to find
The Bride's only BOX was there left behind!

The WILD·THYME they had, and the fuss that was made
Kept the guests in a rout thro' the
DEADLY·NIGHT·SHADE.

But the CLOCKS ticked apace to the ope of
    SNOWFLAKES were fast   DAIS-Y
              falling when all said good-
                                    bye,

With regrets for "that box",–yet they need not to stint,

For the Bridegroom was rich, he'd a post at the MINT

THE HONEYMOON

FINIS